A Kid's Guide to

Origami™

Making
ORIGAMI
TOYS
Step by Step

Michael G. LaFosse

The Rosen Publishing Group's
PowerKids Press™
New York

To the kids at the Pentucket Art Center, Haverhill, Massachusetts

Published in 2002 by The Rosen Publishing Group, Inc.
29 East 21st Street, New York, NY 10010

First Edition

Book Design: Emily Muschinske
Project Editors: Jennifer Landau, Jason Moring, Jennifer Quasha

Illustration Credits: Michael G. LaFosse

Photographs by Cindy Reiman, background image of paper crane on each page © CORBIS.

LaFosse, Michael G.
Making origami toys step by step / Michael G. LaFosse.
    p. cm. — (A kid's guide to origami)
Includes bibliographical references and index.
  ISBN 0-8239-5876-0
1. Origami—Juvenile literature. 2. Paper toy making—Juvenile literature. [1. Origami. 2. Toy making. 3. Handicraft.]
I. Title. II. Series.
  TT870 .L23423 2002
  736'.982—dc21

                                                          2001000163

Manufactured in the United States of America

Contents

What Is Origami?

The art of origami, or paper folding, has been popular in Japan for hundreds of years. In Japanese, "ori" means fold and "kami" means paper. Today people all over the world practice origami. One man who helped make origami popular in recent years is Akira Yoshizawa. Yoshizawa is called the father of modern origami. Origami has a language of **symbols**, just like music. If you know these symbols, you can read an origami book from anywhere in the world.

You don't need to buy special origami paper to make the projects in this book. You can use notepaper, gift wrapping paper, even candy wrappers! Just make sure that the paper is square. The paper also should be the right size for your project. At the start of a project, make sure the origami paper faces in the way that the instructions suggest.

Some projects in this book use more than one sheet of paper. You can make beautiful decorations by combining several folded shapes. Use the origami key on page 22 to help you make your projects. This key also explains terms that are used in some of the projects, such as <u>mountain fold</u> and <u>valley fold</u>.

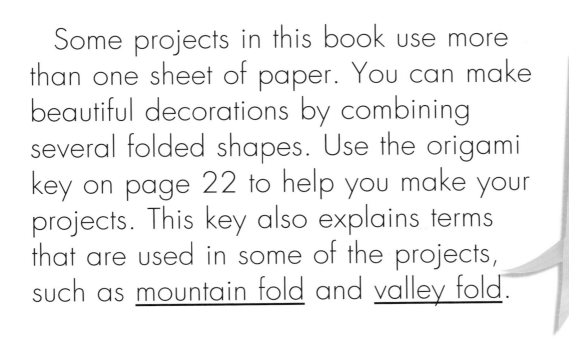

Spinner

Spinning dials and arrows are used often in games of chance. An action usually is required by whomever the spinner points to. Most often the spinner decides whose turn it is. You can use this Spinner to play many kinds of games or just to enjoy watching it spin like a top. You will need a Spinner for other games in this book. It is easy to make a piece of paper into a Spinner. All you have to do is find the center, then make the center the lowest point of the shape. You find the center by making your first two folds!

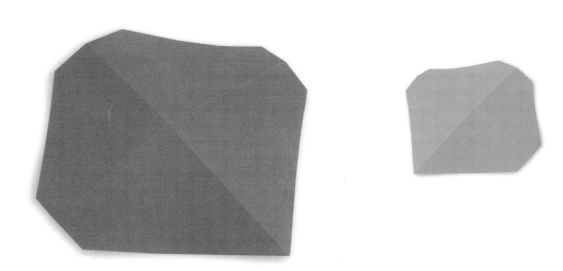

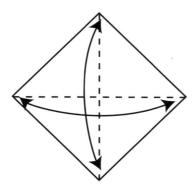

Use a square piece of paper 4 inches (10.2 cm) wide or less. If using origami paper, start with the white side up. Using <u>valley folds</u>, fold in half, corner to corner, each way, and then unfold.

2

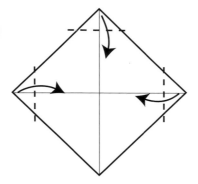

Fold in three of the corners.

3

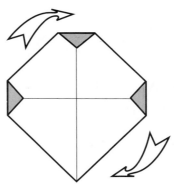

Flick a corner of the paper to make it spin. The colored side should be facing down.

Tower Puzzle

Here is a set of simple paper shapes that you can use to build all kinds of structures. One of the most fun structures to build is a Tower. To make one, you must first construct each of the separate levels, or "floors." Make as many as you think you can use. Stack the levels, one on top of the other. How tall can you make your Tower?

Use the Spinner from the first project to play a building game. Make lots of folded pieces, enough for you and your friends to build a two- or three-level Tower. Each player gets to add a piece to his or her Tower when it is his or her turn. Use the Spinner to see who gets a turn. The first person to complete a Tower wins!

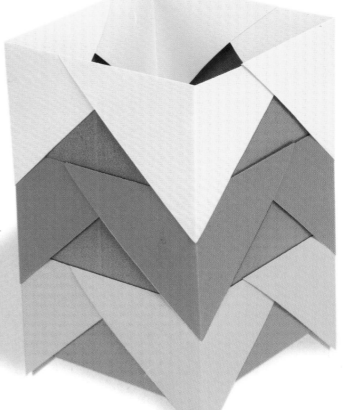

1

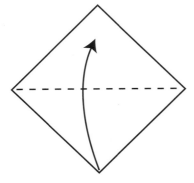

Use eight square pieces of paper 6 inches (15.2 cm) wide or less. If you are using origami paper, start with the white side up. Fold four of the squares of paper in half, corner to corner, to make triangles.

2

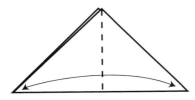

Fold each triangle in half and then unfold.

3

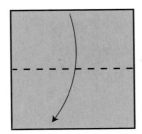

Fold the remaining four papers in half, edge to edge, to make rectangles.

4

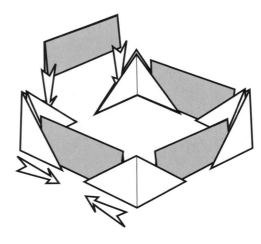

Fit the eight shapes together to make one section. Make more sections and stack them to make a Tower. This plan makes a square form. Try making a triangle form by using only three of each type of section.

Ten Pins

Playing games of skill is a fun way to spend time with friends. Ten Pins is a game of skill in which the player attempts to knock down the most pins with the least number of tries. There are many ways to play this paper version of the game, and you can use more or less than ten Pins. You can make Pins of different colors and can give each color a different number of points. You get the total number of points for the Pins that you knock down in three tries. You can knock down the Pins with a ball of crumpled paper or use the paper Dart from project number four. Use the Spinner from project number one to decide the order of the players.

1

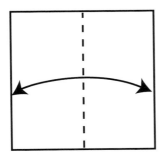

Use square pieces of paper 10 inches (25.4 cm) wide or less. If you are using origami paper, start with the white side up. Fold in half, edge to edge, and unfold.

2

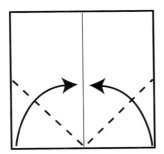

Carefully fold two corners to the crease.

3

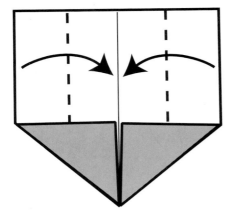

Fold in the two sides.

4

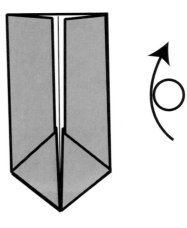

Turn the paper over and open the two flaps to make the Pin stand.

Dart

The great Italian artist and inventor Leonardo da Vinci first came up with the idea for the paper dart about 500 years ago. You can see what it is like to be an inventor by changing the folds of this Dart to make different shapes. Try different shapes and see which fly best.

Paper airplanes fly well when you fold them carefully. Crease your folds very sharply and neatly to make a fast plane. This simple, paper Dart has more paper in the nose than does the **traditional** paper dart. This makes it possible for you to throw the Dart farther. Hold a paper airplane contest and see how far and for how long your planes can fly.

1

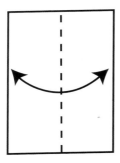

Use an ordinary piece of letter paper. Fold in half, long edge to long edge, then unfold.

2

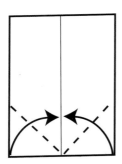

Carefully fold two corners to the crease.

3

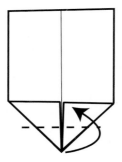

Fold up the bottom point to touch the two paper corners.

4

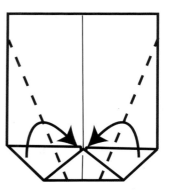

Neatly fold the two short edges into the center.

5

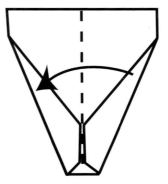

Fold in half.

6

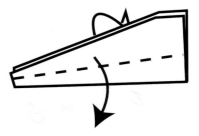

Fold over some paper on each side. Open these layers to shape the wings.

Scoopy Ball

Scoopy Ball is a game of catch that you play with a Ball and a Scoop. You can play this game with many people or by yourself. You will need only one Ball, but you will need one Scoop for each player. Players hold their Scoops at the back where the paper is thicker. The ball can be simply a crumpled piece of paper or a piece of wrapped candy.

There are many ways to play Scoopy Ball, and you can make up new rules. Try to toss the Ball from player to player using only the Scoop to throw and catch. Any player who misses the Ball gets a point. The player with the lowest score at the end of the game wins.

1

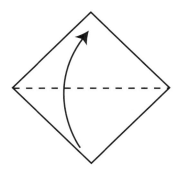

Use a square piece of paper 10 inches (25.4 cm) wide or less. If you are using origami paper, start with the colored side up. Fold in half, corner to corner.

2

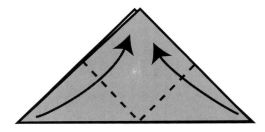

Fold up the bottom corners carefully so that they touch the top corner.

3

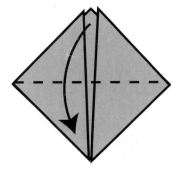

Fold down the two corners to touch the bottom corner.

4

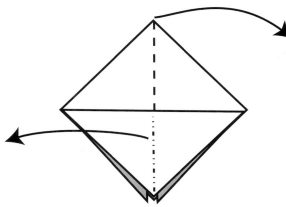

Open the paper to form a Scoop.

Stacking Wings

This design is great for a **celebration**. Make at least six or more Wings for each hand and toss them all in the air at once. The Wings will loop, zip, and dart in all directions. Use colorful papers to make the Wings look their best. They will look kind of like **hang gliders**. These Wings can be stacked neatly on top of each other because of their shape. No matter how you get these little Wings into the air, they will fly. The extra layers of paper in the "nose" of the Wing make it **denser** there. The denser part of the paper moves faster than the rest so it is always in front. That is how the nose knows which way to go. Throw a single Wing in the air over your head and watch how the Wing falls, nose first.

1

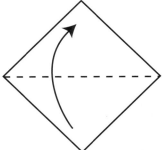

Use square pieces of paper 6 inches (15.2 cm) wide. If you are using origami paper, start with the colored side up. Fold in half, corner to corner, to make a triangle.

2

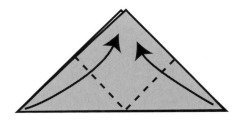

Fold up the bottom corners carefully so that they touch the top corner.

3

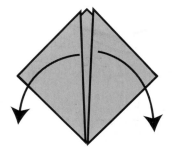

Return the two corners to the bottom.

4

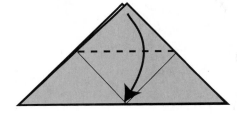

Fold down the top corner to touch the middle of the bottom edge.

5

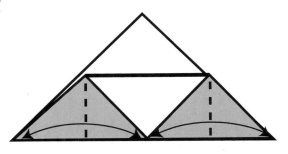

Fold in the bottom corners to meet at the middle of the bottom edge. Unfold.

6

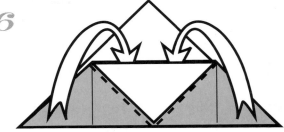

Tuck in the bottom corners.

7

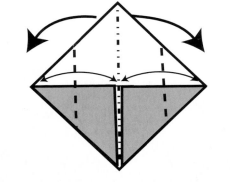

Fold the side corners to the center and unfold. Make a <u>mountain fold</u> up the middle. Turn over the paper.

Jumping Frog

This Frog really jumps! It has a big mouth, too! What do you suppose that a Frog like this would eat? Maybe it would eat origami flies?

You can play a game of skill to see how many Frogs you can make jump into a cup in 1 minute. You will need a watch or a clock to keep track of the time. You can use a single Tower level from project number two instead of a cup. Make a bunch of Frogs and have a try. See who can make their Frogs jump the highest or the farthest. You can use any kind of paper to make Frogs, but smaller papers and stiffer papers make the best jumpers.

1

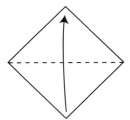

Use a square piece of paper 6 inches (15.2 cm) wide or less. If you are using origami paper, start with the white side up. Fold in half, bottom corner to top corner, to make a triangle.

2

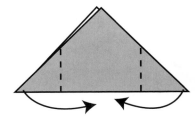

Fold in the left and right corners to meet at the middle of the bottom edge.

3

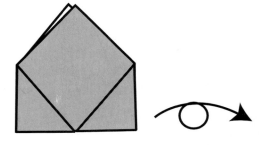

Turn over the paper.

4

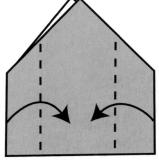

Fold in the left and right edges to meet in the middle.

5

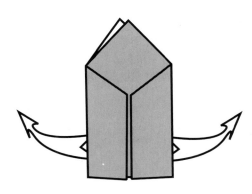

Bring out the two corners from the back.

6

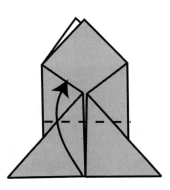

Fold up the bottom edge, just to the level of the two corners.

7

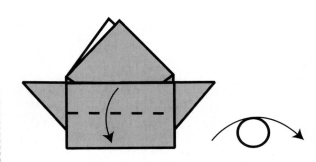

Fold down the edge to the bottom. Turn over the paper.

Fishing Game

This game of skill calls for patience and a steady hand. Make as many Fish as you like and then make a fishing pole from a pencil, a string, and a paper clip. Tie one end of the string to the pencil and the other end to the paper clip. Bend open the last turn of the paper clip to form the hook. Catch Fish by hooking the Fish's loops.

You and your friends can take turns trying to catch Fish. Set a time limit and see who catches the most during his or her turn. Write numbers on the backs of the Fish to give them different point values. Add the points to see who scores the highest.

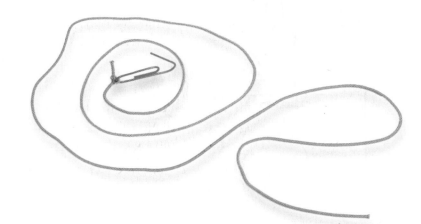

1

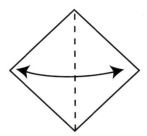

Use square paper 6 inches (15.2 cm) wide or less. If you are using origami paper, start with the white side up. Fold in half, corner to corner, and unfold.

2

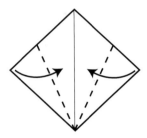

Carefully fold two edges to the crease to make a kite shape.

3

Fold down the two square corners.

4

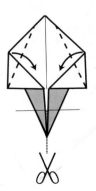

Cut a small slit at the bottom point where the tail will be. Fold in the top edges, but not all the way to the center. Look at drawing number five to see the correct shape.

5

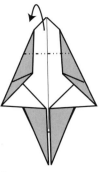

Mountain fold the top point around the back.

6

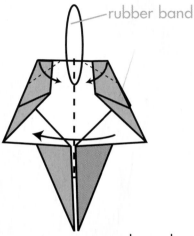

Fold in the top two corners and attach a rubber band or a loop of string with glue or tape. Fold in half.

7

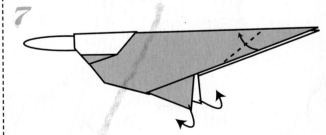

Move the paper to look like this. Fold up the front layer of the tail paper to make the tail fin. Fold out the two fins on the belly to the sides. Give the tail a curve to make it look like it is swimming.

Origami Key

1. MOUNTAIN FOLD

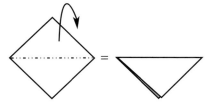

mountain-fold line

To make a mountain fold, hold the paper so the white side is facing up. Fold the top corner back (away from you) to meet the bottom corner.

2. VALLEY FOLD

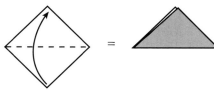

valley-fold line

To make a valley fold, hold the paper so the white side is facing up. Fold the bottom corner up to meet the top corner.

3. TURN OVER

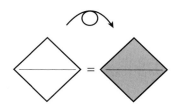

4. ROTATE

5. MOVE or PUSH

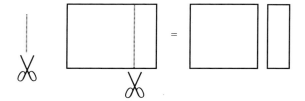

6. CUT

7. FOLD and UNFOLD

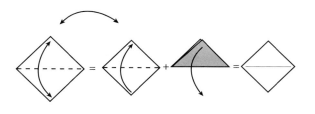

8. DIRECTION ARROW

Glossary

celebration (seh-luh-BRAY-shun) A party or event that marks a special occasion.

denser (DENS-er) Closer together, thicker.

hang gliders (HANG GLY-derz) Gliders like large kites. The people riding them hold on to frames underneath the wings and take off from a cliff or hilltop.

symbols (SIM-bulz) Objects or designs that stand for something else.

traditional (truh-DIH-shuh-nul) Following the way things are usually done.

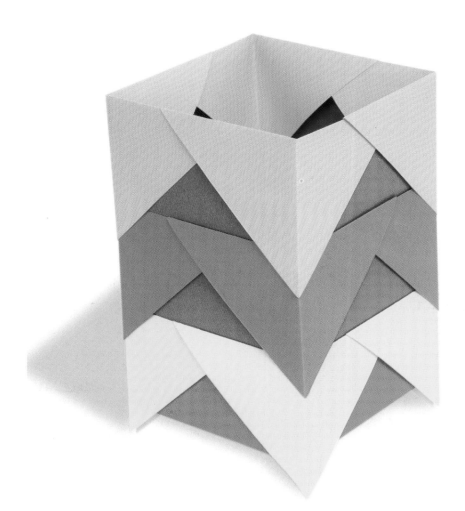

Index

Web Sites

To find out more about origami, check out these Web sites:

www.origamido.com
www.origami-usa.org